•••• BULLETPOINTS ••••

HORSES & PONIES

Marion Curry

Miles Kelly

PUBLISHING

First published in 2005 by Miles Kelly Publishing Ltd
Bardfield Centre, Great Bardfield
Essex, CM7 4SL

2 4 6 8 10 9 7 5 3 1

Editorial Director: Belinda Gallagher
Editorial Assistant: Hannah Todd **Designer:** Neil Sargent, DPI Colour
Picture Research: Liberty Newton **Production:** Estela Boulton

British Library Cataloguing-in-Publication Data
A catalogue record for this book is available from the British Library

ISBN 1-84236-531-2

Printed in China

www.mileskelly.net
info@mileskelly.net

The publishers would like to thank the following artists who have contributed to this book:
Steve Caldwell (Allied Artists), Jim Channel, Terry Gabbey, Sally Holmes, Richard Hook (Linden Artists),
Janos Marffy, Angus McBride, Andrea Morandi, Terry Riley, Peter Sarson, Rudi Vizi,
Mike White (Temple Rogers)

The publishers would like to thank the following sources for the use of their photographs:
Page 4 Acquire Image Media; 6 Bob Langrish; 10, 14, 16 Acquire Image Media; 17 Lisa Clayden; 18 (Evergreen Hamlet)
Nicholas Pound; 19 (Moorcorner Minstrel II) Nicholas Pound; 20 (Lowhouses Black Magic) Nipna Stud; 21(Inglegarth
Illustrious/Townend Aaron) Janice Boyd; 22, 32 Bob Langrish; 37 (Kvaals Aida) Dawn Thorpe

All other pictures are from: Miles Kelly Archives; Corel;
DigitalSTOCK; digitalvision; PhotoDisc

Contents

Arab 4

Quarter Horse 6

Thoroughbred 8

Shire and Clydesdale 10

Welsh Ponies and Cobs 12

Highland and Shetland 14

Dartmoor and Exmoor 16

Connemara and
    New Forest 18

Fell and Dales 20

Akhal-Teke 22

Haflinger and Icelandic 24

Appaloosa and Dutch
    Warmblood 26

Andalucian and
    Lipizzaner 28

Tennesse Walking Horse
    and Morgan 30

Cleveland Bay and
    Hanoverian 32

Mustang, Paint and
    Pinto 34

Other pony breeds 36

Other horse breeds 38

Index 40

Arab

- **The Arabian Horse**, or Arab, is the oldest pure-bred horse in the world. Its head is small, with a dished face, large eyes, and a thin muzzle.

  - **The Arabian** was the horse of the Bedouin people – nomadic Arabs – as early as 3000 to 2500BC. They were later introduced into Europe.

    - **This ancient breed** is widely regarded as the definition of beauty and elegance in horses. Famed for its speed, strength, and endurance, the Arab has influenced the development of almost all modern horse breeds.

    - **Arabs** usually stand 14 hh to 15.2 hh.

    - **Arabs are intelligent**, sensitive and courageous creatures. They are also loyal, if well-treated, and enjoy attention.

      - **Among the horses** that carried their famous riders into battle wcre Napoleon's Marengo, Alexander the Great's Bucephalus, and the Duke of Wellington's Copenhagen.

      - **The earliest Arab horse** brought to the US was a stallion called Ranger, which arrived in 1765. It is said to have sired the horse George Washington rode during the American Revolutionary War.

◀ *The Arab has been used to improve the stock of other horse breeds throughout history. An Anglo-Arab is a cross between a Thoroughbred and a pure-bred Arab.*

▲ *At rest, an Arab horse's tail may trail on the ground, but when in action the tail is held high in the air.*

- **The action** of the Arab is unique and the breed is characterized by a 'floating' movement – covering the maximum amount of ground with the minimum of effort.

- **During the Crimean War** (1851–54), one Arab horse raced 93 mi (153 km) without harm, but its rider died from exhaustion.

> **FASCINATING FACT**
> The anatomy of the Arab horse is unique
> – it has 17 ribs, one less than other breeds.

Quarter Horse

▼ *The agility and speed of the Quarter Horse makes it ideal for ranch work.*

- **The breed** got its name because it was bred to race short distances – no more than a quarter of a mile. It is is the oldest all-American breed.

- **Quarter Horses** measure between 14 hh to 16 hh. They may be any whole colour, but are mainly chestnut.

- **Powerful and muscular** conformation gives the Quarter Horse speed, ability and balance.

- **The breed** was developed by English colonists in the early 1600s.

- **Known for** its 'cow sense' – the ability to outmanoeuvre cattle – and calm disposition, the Quarter Horse was ideally suited for the challenge of the West.

- **The breed** is renowned for its versatility and excellent temperament.

- **The Quarter Horses is North America's** favourite breed with over two million listed by the American Quarter Horse Association and another 800,000 members worldwide.

- **The American Quarter Horse Association** was formed in 1940.

- **Quarter Horses** are used in western riding competitions, demonstrations and rodeo.

> **FASCINATING FACT**
> Peter McCue, born in 1895 in Illinois, USA,
> is the most famous breed stallion, credited with
> establishing the modern Quarter Horse.

Thoroughbred

- **The Thoroughbred** horse stands 15 hh to 16.2 hh.

- **The history** of the Thoroughbred and the birth of the racing industry are interlinked.

- **The introduction** of Arab blood increased the speed and endurance of the breed. They are now the most famous racehorses in the world.

- **Racing is called** 'The Sport of Kings' because it was the English kings of the 15th century who encouraged the development of racing and breeding of Thoroughbreds.

▲ *Thoroughbred racing is popular sport. Different levels and lengths of race are held worldwide.*

- **The first Thoroughbred** arrived in America in 1730.

- **Thoroughbreds are usually whole colours**, especially bay, chestnut and brown and often grey, black and roan. Many have white markings.

- **Three famous stallions**, Byerley Turk, the Darley Arabian and the Godolphin Arab are seen as the founders of the Thoroughbred breed.

- **Thoroughbreds are often unsuited** to inexperienced riders as they can be temperamental and may overreact to events. Horse that retire from the racing industry require careful rehabilitation and rehoming, but can be successful hunters and three-day eventers.

FASCINATING FACT
Thoroughbreds can begin their racing
career at just two years old.

● **Thoroughbreds** are often crossed with other breeds. These half- or part-bred animals make excellent competition horses in both the showing and showjumping world. Their influence has been used to improve breeds throughout the world.

▶ *The initials TB stand for Thoroughbred, while the term half-bred describes a horse who has only one parent that is a Thoroughbred.*

Shire and Clydesdale

- **One of the largest horses** in the world, the Shire, originated in England and is a descendant of the Old English Black Horse whose ancestors were the great horses of medieval times.

- **The Shire stands up to** 18 hh, and may be bay, brown, black or grey.

- **Shires still work** the land in some parts of Britain and several brewers use them to pull drays in the city streets.

- **Shire numbers** dropped into the thousands after World War II but today there is a renewed interest in the breed. They are used as draught horses and bred with Thoroughbreds to make heavyweight hunters.

- **The Shire Horse Society** was founded in 1878 to 'promote the old English breed of cart horse'.

- **Clydesdales** are a breed of heavy draught horse, recognized for their strength, style, and versatility. The breed originated from Scottish farm horses over 200 years ago.

◄ *The mane and tails are ornately decorated for showing classes.*

- **Clydesdales** were not only used as pulling power on farms, but also transported goods within and between towns. They can pull many times more than their own weight, which is why the breed was so popular for transporting goods by wagon.

- **Clydesdales** can grow to over 18 hh. They are usually bay or brown in colour with four white legs and a mass of soft feathers about the feet.

- **The Clydesdale** was the first draught horse in Great Britain to have an individual society. The Clydesdale Horse Society was founded in 1877. In 1911, 1617 stallions were exported from Great Britain.

- **Although no longer** required to work on farms, the breed is now popular for showing and breeding.

▶ *These shires horses are shown in harness as a working pair. This breed should have a slightly Roman or convex nose and large and set wide eyes.*

Welsh Ponies and Cobs

● **The Welsh breed** is split into four sections: A, B, C and D.

● **The original** and smallest of the Welsh breeds is the Welsh Mountain Pony (Section A). It stands no more than 12 hh and is most commonly grey – although it can be any colour except piebald and skewbald. The head should be small with neat pointed ears, big bold eyes and a wide forehead.

▲ *The Welsh Cob makes an excellent driving pony*

- **Section B** is the Welsh Pony. These ponies were used by farmers to herd sheep and other ponies. Today the breed is mainly used as riding ponies for children. They are shown and ridden in jumping competitions.

- **Section C** is the Welsh Pony of Cob type. This pony is stronger than the Welsh Pony and was originally used for farm work. A versatile breed, they are ideal for both for riding and driving.

- **Section D** is the Welsh Cob and the tallest of the breed. These cobs are noted for courage and endurance and are strong and agile.

- **The Welsh Ponies** and Cobs (Section B, C and D) have the same colouring as the Welsh Mountain Pony (Section A).

- **The Welsh Section B and C** do not exceed 13.2 hh. Welsh Section D cobs exceed 13.2 hh.

- **Welsh Ponies** and Cobs are renowned for being sure-footed, hardy and natural jumpers.

- **The Welsh Pony and Cob Society** was established in 1901 and published the first volume of the Welsh Stud Book in 1902.

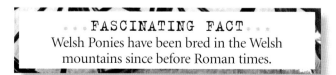

FASCINATING FACT
Welsh Ponies have been bred in the Welsh mountains since before Roman times.

Highland and Shetland

- **The Shetland** and Highland pony breeds both originate from the far north of the British Isles.

- **Native to** the Shetland Islands off northern Scotland, the Shetland is the smallest British native pony. The breed standard states that they should not be any taller than 42 in (107 cm) high. They are generally measured in inches or centimetres rather than hands. Shetlands were originally used as working ponies carrying peat and seaweed.

  - **There are miniature** Shetland Ponies that should not exceed 34 in (87 cm) high.

    - **Shetland Ponies** can be of any colour except spotted. The breed has a double coat with guard hairs in winter to help keep out the wind and rain. They also have particularly thick manes and tails to help keep them warm. In summer, they develop a short, shiny coat.

    - **The Shetland** is an extremely strong pony, and is thought to be the strongest of all breeds for its size.

    - **There have been Shetland Ponies** on the Shetland Islands for over 2000 years. Over the past 200 years, they have been exported all over the world.

◀ *Shetland ponies were used as pit ponies in the mining industry, but are now popular for driving, showing and as children's ponies.*

- **The Highland** is the largest of the Scottish breeds, standing between 12 hh and 14 hh.

- **The breed originated** in the Highlands of Scotland. There are two types: the Mainland, which is larger, and the smaller Island Pony.

- **Highland ponies** come in a variety of colours including dun, brown, bay and black and Highland Ponies bred on the island of Rhum show unusual colours, such as chestnut with a silver mane.

- **Crofters used Highland Ponies** for haulage and farm work, and they are still used on many hunting estates to transport deer and game. Highland Ponies are also used for trekking, riding for the disabled and as all-round family ponies.

▲ *The Highland is an ancient breed that can survive on scarce grazing.*

15

Dartmoor and Exmoor

▲ *The Dartmoor Pony is the symbol of the Dartmoor National Park.*

- **The Dartmoor** is a small pony no bigger than 12.2 hh and is usually coloured black, bay or brown.

- **The ancient breed** is native to Dartmoor in Devon, England.

- **Dartmoor** is an exposed area of moorland standing over 300 m (1000 ft) above sea level. This has resulted in the breed evolving into a hardy, sure-footed pony which can survive on limited grazing.

- **Dartmoor Ponies** are particularly noted for their calm temperament and lack of excitability, making them suitable for children to ride and look after. They are also ideal for driving and showing.

FASCINATING FACT
Until the 1960s, Dartmoor Ponies were used to escort inmates from the local prison whilst on outside duties.

- **As well as being used** on farms Dartmoor Ponies have been used to transport tin from the mines.

- **The Exmoor Pony** has inhabited the Exmoor moorland of southwest Britain for many years. They are brown, bay or dun coloured with lighter mealy-coloured markings around their eyes and muzzles. They stand at about 12 hh.

- **Exmoor ponies** are thought to have existed since prehistoric times, but are now a very rare breed. Today there is thought to be less than 200 ponies living on Exmoor.

- **In the past**, farmers used Exmoor Ponies for agricultural work and shepherding. They are very strong and able to carry adult riders easily.

- **Because of its strength** the Exmoor is not ideally suited for children who are beginning to ride, but with a competent rider they can take part in showing, jumping and long-distance riding.

▲ *Exmoor ponies are described as having 'toad' eyes. This means their eyes are hooded.*

17

Connemara and New Forest

- **The Connemara** is the only native pony of Ireland. They are usually grey, black, brown or dun and occasionally roan, chestnut or palomino, measuring between 13 hh and 14.2 hh.

- **Connemara Ponies** were mostly used by farmers to transport heavy goods, such as peat, potatoes and seaweed and pull a trap for family transport. Today, they are used as children's ponies, and for competing, driving and showing.

- **Connemaras are intelligent** and willing, as well as agile and obedient.

- **Hardy**, athletic and with good balance, the Connemara is also strong and free-moving.

◀ *The Connemara makes an excellent competition pony for teenagers or small adults.*

- **The Connemara breed** is often crossed with the Thoroughbred or Arab. These part-bred horses make successful competition horses in dressage, showjumping and three-day eventing.

- **The New Forest Pony** comes from southern England, where it can still be found living wild in the New Forest region. They are usually bay, brown or grey, standing 12 hh to 14.2 hh and make excellent riding ponies.

- **The New Forest** Breeding and Cattle Society produced its first stud book in 1960. The breed rules permit any colour except piebald, skewbald or blue-eyed cream.

- **New Forest Ponies** are naturally sure-footed and hardy.

- **A long smooth stride** makes New Forest Ponies comfortable to ride and they are ideal for trekking and endurance.

▶ *A quality New Forest Pony excels in the show ring.*

Fell and Dales

▶ *The Dales Pony combines good conformation with energy and ability, making the breed ideal for riding and driving.*

- **Fell and Dales** pony breeds originated in the north of England. The two breeds are genetically related, with the Fell being slightly smaller and lighter in build than the Dales.

- **Dales Ponies** on average stand between 13.2 hh and 14.2 hh. They are mostly black, but there are also bays and a few greys.

- **In the 19th century**, Dales Ponies were used for agricultural work and to carry lead from mines to the ports. They are known as good trotters with considerable stamina and a docile temperament.

- **Dales Ponies** are often used as trekking ponies as they are capable of carrying adults.They are also popular for general-riding, showing and driving.

- **The Dales Pony** almost became extinct in the 1950s, but numbers increased after the formation of the Dales Pony Society in 1963.

- **Fell Ponies** were traditionally used as pack ponies carrying lead from the mines. They were also used for pulling carts and trotting races.

- **Fell Ponies** vary in height between 13 hh and 14 hh.

- **The breed standards** of the Fell Pony allow black, brown, bay or grey, preferably with no white markings. They have long manes and tails, and silky feathering on their legs.

- **Fell Ponies** are an old breed, dating back to Roman times when they were used as draught animals.

- **Fell Ponies** are renowned for their good paces. Their active walk and fast trot makes them an ideal driving pony.

▼ *The constitution of the Fell Pony is said to be 'as hard as iron'.*

Akhal-Teke

- **The Akhal-Teke** is an ancient breed that dates back over 3000 years.

- **The breed originated** from the Turkoman Steppes in Central Asia and takes its name from a nomadic tribe known as Teke found at the Akhal oasis.

- **The average height** is between 14.2 hh and 15.2 hh and an Akhal-Teke may be dun, bay, chestnut, grey or black with a short and silky tail. The head of an Akhal-Teke is similar to an Arab's and its body is described as one of the most elegant in the horse world.

- **The breed** is noted for stamina and endurance. This was shown in 1935 when a group of Akhal-Teke horses were taken on a three-day trek across the desert to Moscow without water.

- **Developed to suit** desert conditions the Akhal-Teke horse has fine skin with a long back and narrow quarters.

- **Today,** they are used in many different disciplines including racing and endurance.

- **In history** Akhal-Teke have been prized by Alexander the Great, Genghis Khan and Marco Polo. Alexander the Great even erected a tomb to commemorate his Akhal-Teke stallion, Bucephalus.

- **The Turkmenistan's** national emblem features the breed.

- **The rider of an Akhal-Teke** needs to be confident and calm as they are known to have sensitive natures and to dislike strangers.

FASCINATING FACT
The Akhal-Teke has been used as a racehorse for over 3000 years

▼ *This herd of Akhal-Teke horses show the wide range of colours common to their breed.*

Haflinger and Icelandic

- **A pony standing** between 13.1 hh and 14.2 hh, the Haflinger is palomino or chestnut with a light-coloured mane and tail. The breed takes its name from the village of Haflinger near the border of Austria and Italy.

- **The Haflinger** is a small, strong pony. It has a slightly dished face and large eyes, and enjoys exercise.

- **Haflingers** make good riding ponies, but are very versatile and can be used for driving, endurance and even as vaulting ponies for acrobatic displays. They have also proved a popular breed with centres for disabled riders because of their honest, calm natures.

- **Haflingers** are now established around the world and a register of pure-bred Haflinger stallions has been kept for over 100 years.

- **As there is no word** for pony in Icelandic, the Icelandic, although under 13.2 hh, is always referred to as a horse.

- **Icelandic horses** have three layers to their coats to help them withstand the harsh climate in which they live.

- **The Icelandic breed** is long-lived, and an animal is not considered mature until seven years old.

- **Icelandic horses** can be of any colour, have a stocky build and are noted for good eyesight and tough nature.

- **The horses still play** a large part in Icelandic life. As well as being excellent family riding horses, they compete in showing, endurance, and special race meetings.

FASCINATING FACT
In Italy in 2003 the first cloned horse
was born to a Haflinger mare.

▼ *Haflingers are small and
strong. They are a hardy breed
ideally suited to working on
mountain slopes.*

25

Appaloosa and Dutch Warmblood

- **The Appaloosa** is an ancient breed depicted in prehistoric cave paintings. It is known for its spotted coat that comes in a variety of recognized patterns, but the breed can also have whole colour coats. The main patterns are known as blanket, spots, leopard, snowflake and frost. They often have black-and-white markings on their feet.

- **The base colour** of an Appaloosa's coat can be a variety of different colours, including bay, black, chestnut and palomino. They have short manes and tails and usually stand between 14.2 hh and 16 hh.

▼ *Over 500,000 Appaloosas are registered in the Appaloosa Horse Club today. The club was established in 1938.*

- **In the US**, Appaloosas were developed by the Nez Perce – Native American Indians who lived in north-west America. The breed was virtually destroyed in the late 1800s when the US army captured the Nez Perce Indians and killed their horses.

- **The word Appaloosa** is derived from Palouse country, an area surrounding the Palouse River. Today, Appaloosas are prized for endurance riding, because of their strength and strong limbs.

- **The Dutch Warmblood** originated in Holland and usually stands between 15.2 hh and 17 hh.

- **Dutch Warmbloods** are usually chestnut, bay, black or grey with white markings on the face and legs.

- **There are two distinct types** of Dutch Warmbloods: the heavier horse, called a Groningen, which is used in agriculture, and the lighter Gelderland, which is a driving and riding horse that also excels in showjumping.

- **Initially used** by farmers for agricultural work, Dutch Warmbloods have been subjected to strict breeding programmes to encourage the best conformation possible.

- **The Gelderlander** is recognized as a brilliant sports performance horse.

> **FASCINATING FACT**
> All Appaloosa foals are born with light coats
> that eventually grow darker. However, greys start
> dark and become lighter.

Andalucian and Lipizzaner

- **The Andalucian** stands between 15 hh and 16.2 hh. The breed originates from Spain and was the chosen warhorse of the Spanish conquistadors.

- **Andalucian coats** are usually grey or black, but can also be dun and palomino. One of their coat colours is called mulberry – a dappled grey with hints of purple. The breed has strong rear quarters with thick manes and tails.

- **The Andalucian breed** is noted for its intelligence, beauty and sensitivity and they can make excellent dressage horses.

- **In medieval times**, Andalucian horses were bred and protected by Carthusian monks.

- **In Spain**, Andalucians are called *pura espagnol* or 'pure Spanish horses'.

- **Lipizzaners are used** at The Spanish Riding School of Vienna – the oldest riding school in the world. These horses are taught special movements, involving controlled athletic jumps and kicks known as 'airs above ground'. The movements are said to be based on medieval tricks of war that were used to evade enemy soldiers.

- **Lipizzaners** usually have grey coats. The foals are born black or brown and develop their grey coats as they mature. This can take as long as ten years.

- **The ancestry** of the Lipizzaner dates back to AD800. They are a result of crossing Berber horses from North Africa with horses used by the Romans for chariot racing known as Karst horses.

- **Archduke Charles II of Austria** founded a special stud at Lipizza (Lipica) in 1580 to produce the best horses possible from where the Lipizzaner breed takes its name.

- **One of the most famous** movements performed by the Lipizzaner during displays is the *ballotade*. The horse leaps into the air while keeping its legs tucked underneath it.

▶ *A Lipizzaner demonstrating the* levade *where it takes its weight on the hind quarters in a controlled manner while raising the upper body and tucking in its front legs.*

Tennessee Walking Horse and Morgan

- **Roy Rogers**, the famous television cowboy, rode a Tennessee Walking Horse called Trigger. This breed has a particular gait that resembles a running walk.

- **Tennessee Walking Horses** range in size from 15 hh to 17 hh and come in a variety of colours, including black, bay or chestnut.

▶ *Morgans are popular ridden showhorses.*

- **With long tails** that are high set and a deep muscular chest, Tennessee Walking Horses are said to be particularly calm and good-natured horses.

- **The first horse** to develop the gliding walk was born in 1837. This trait was developed by farmers and plantation owners in Tennessee who wanted a horse capable of covering long distances with a smooth stride. Some Tennessee Walking Horses are said to click their teeth in time to the rhythm of the walk.

- **The Tennessee Walking Horse** has become so popular that it is one of the top ten breeds recognized in the US.

- **The Morgan** originates from Vermont in the US and dates back to the 18th century. The breed can be traced back to one stallion who took its name from its owner, Justin Morgan.

- **On average** Morgans stand between 14.1 hh and 15.2 hh. They are primarily brown, bay, black or chestnut.

- **The eyes** should be large and prominent and its shapely ears set wide apart. Mares often have longer ears than stallions.

- **The breed** is noted for strength and particularly gentle temperament.

- **The Morgan Horse Club** was founded in 1909 to stop the decline in the breed. Today, they compete in many disciplines including showing, dressage, jumping and driving.

Cleveland Bay and Hanoverian

- **The Cleveland Bay** is the oldest breed of English horse.

- **Cleveland Bays** stand between 15.3 hh and 17 hh, and as the name suggests are bay coloured, without feathering on the legs. They take their name from the area of North England where they were originally bred.

- **In the mid-eighteenth century**, Cleveland Bays were known as Chapman horses. Chapmen were early travelling salesmen who used the horses to transport their goods. They were also used in agriculture. They are known to live a long time and mature at about six years old.

◄ *Cleveland Bays make excellent driving horses because of their good temperament and endurance.*

- **Cleveland Bays** are intelligent with good temperament and were popular carriage horses. They were used by the British cavalry in the World War I and even today British royalty use them to pull state coaches.

- **The Cleveland Bay** is often crossed with the Thoroughbred – the resulting part-bred animal makes an excellent competition horse.

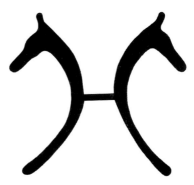

▲ *The identifying 'H' brand mark of a pure Hanoverian.*

- **The Hanoverian** originates from Germany. A tall horse, the breed stands between 16 hh and 17 hh and may come in any solid colour.

- **The excellent gaits** of the Hanoverian include a ground covering walk, a free-moving trot and a rhythmic canter.

- **Originally** Hanoverians were bred for the military and as strong carriage horses. They are noted for their strong backs.

- **Hanoverians are now bred** as performance horses and are winners at Olympic level in showjumping and dressage. They also excel in driving and eventing.

> ... **FASCINATING FACT** ...
> It is believed Cleveland Bays evolved from
> the horses left in Britain by the Romans.

Mustang, Paint and Pinto

- **The word Mustang** is derived from a Spanish word meaning 'stray' or 'ownerless'.

- **Mustang horses** were introduced to the US around the 1700s by Spanish settlers, but animals were abandoned and broke free to form huge herds that numbered about two million by 1900.

- **In order to protect** grassland grazing for cattle, the Mustangs were culled and by 1970 their numbers were reduced to less than 17,000. They are now a protected breed and their numbers are managed.

◀ *The Pinto horse was first introduced into North America by Spanish explorers.*

- **Mustangs** stand between 13 hh and 16 hh and can be of any colour.

- **Mustangs were used** by both the Native American Indians and cowboys.

- **American Paint Horses** are clearly defined by both coat patterning and conformation. They have to come from stock recognized by the American Paint Horse Association, the American Quarter Horse Association or the Jockey Club. Their coats are a mixture of white and any other colour.

- **There are three** recognized coat patterns for Paint Horses called Tobiano, Overo and Tovero. The patterns relate to how the pattern of markings covers the horse's body and legs. For example, the Tobiano generally has white legs and the Overo usually has one or more dark coloured legs.

- **The Paint Horse** is valued as being a strong versatile horse that excels both as a leisure riding horse and in competition.

- **The Pinto horse** was associated with the North American Indians and was believed to have special magical powers in battle.

- **The Pinto Horse Association of America** recognizes different breeds and cross-breeds as long as they have the required colouring.

Other pony breeds

- **Przewalski's Horse** takes its name from a Russian explorer, Colonel Nikolai Przewalski, who is said to have discovered the breed in Mongolia in 1881. A small stubborn breed, it stands between 12 hh and 14 hh and is dun coloured with a dorsal stripe along the back and zebra stripes on the legs. It has an erect mane and dark brown tail.

- **Camargue Ponies** originate from Southern France. Many still live in wild herds on salt marshes in the Camargue region.

- **The rare Eriskay Pony** is an ancient breed found on the island of Eriskay in the Hebrides, off Scotland. These hardy ponies were originally used by crofters to carry peat and seaweed.

- **Chinoteagues** are the only pony native to the US. They stand about 12 hh and are extremely hardy, able to survive on little vegetation. A number of wild ponies still live on the islands off the Virginian coast.

◀ *The extravagant action of the Hackney makes him unsuitable as a riding pony, but excellent as a driving pony.*

▶ *Fjord Ponies traditionally have their coarse manes trimmed in a crescent shape with the dark central hair left slightly longer.*

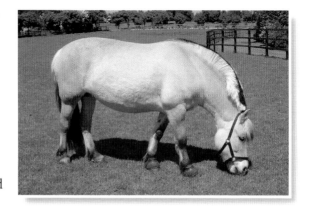

- **The Fjord Pony** was used in battle by the Vikings and also for ploughing. They are striking-looking ponies, standing 14 hh and 14.2 hh, dun coloured with a dorsal stripe.

- **The Hackney** is a showy, high-stepping horse or pony. The pony stands under 14 hh – the horse 14 hh to 16 hh.

- **The Newfoundland Pony** developed from a cross of British native ponies. Standing 11 hh to 14.2 hh, they are usually brown with a thick mane and tail. Over recent decades, their numbers have dipped and efforts are being made to increase the population.

- **The Caspian** is one of the oldest equine breeds. These small ponies stand up to 12 hh and are bold and fast-moving, making them ideal for competitive scurry driving.

- **The Konik Pony** is widespread throughout Poland and in rural areas is still used in agricultural work.

> **FASCINATING FACT**
> Camargue Ponies are usually grey and are known as the 'white horse of the sea'.

Other horse breeds

- **The American Standardbred** is the most popular harness racer in the world. The name 'Standardbred' was used because horses had to reach a certain standard over a mile to be registered as part of the new breed.

- **The Brabant**, or Belgium Heavy Draught, is descended from the medieval heavy war horse. It is the most popular draught breed in the US. These large horses stand between 16 hh and 18 hh and are usually chestnut or roan with light manes and tails.

- **The Trakehner** stands between 16 hh and 16.2 hh and can be any colour. The breed originates from Prussia where a stud was established in 1732.

- **The Percheron** is a strong, heavyweight horse, standing 15 hh to 17 hh. Usually grey or black in colour, this breed originated in France and has developed into one of the strongest draught horses in the world.

- **The Yili** from China is a new breed, developed from crossing Russian horses with native stock. They are described as draught/riding horses standing about 14 hh and usually bay in colour. They can cover long distances at speed because of their excellent stamina.

▲ *Percherons have broad chests with strong forearms and excellent feet.*

- **The Canadian Horse** is renowned for its stamina, versatility and willingness to please. Because of their hardiness, they became known as the 'little iron horse'. They are usually black, standing 14 hh to 16 hh and have docile characters.

- **American Saddlebred** horses usually stands at around 16 hh. They are popular riding and driving horses.

- **The Falabella** is the best-known miniature horse breed. They are usually about 76 cm (30 in) tall at the withers.

- **Mostly chestnut** and standing over 16 hh, the versatile Selle Français is successful as an all-round competition horse. Its name means 'French saddle horse'.

- **The Holsteiner** is one of Germany's oldest warmblood breeds and is successful in all spheres of competition.

▶ *The American Saddlebred is a specialist breed that has a high-stepping action and is a popular show horse.*

Index

A, Welsh Section 12
Akhal-Teke breed **22–23**, *22–23*
American
  Paint breed **34–35**
  Association 35
  Association 7, 35
  Saddlebred breed **39**, *39*
  Standardbred breed **38**
Andalucian breed **28–29**
Anglo-Arab cross *4*
Appaloosa, breed **26–27**, *26*
Arab horse, breed **4–5**, *4, 5*

B, Welsh Section 12
Belgium Heavy Draught breed **38**
Berber horses 28
Brabant breed **38**
breeds
  horse **38–39**
  pony **36–37**
Bucephalus 4, 23
Byerley Turk 8

C, Welsh Section 12
Camargue breed **36–37**
Canadian Horse breed **39**
Carthusians 28
Caspian breed **37**
Chapman horses 32
Chinoteague breed **36**
Cleveland Bay breed **32–33**, *32*
cloning, horses *24*
Clydesdale breed **10–11**
Clydesdale Horse Society 11
coat
  double 14
  three-layered 24
Connemara breed **18–19**, *18*

D, Welsh Section 12
Dales breed **20–21**, *20*
Dales Pony Society 20
Darley Arabian 8
Dartmoor 16
  breed **16–17**, *16*
draught horse breeds 10–11, **38–39**
dressage
  Andalucian 28
  Morgan 31
Dutch Warmblood breed **26–27**

endurance riding
  Akhal-Teke 23
  New Forest 19
Eriskay breed **36**
Exmoor breed **16–17**, *17*

Falabella breed **39**
feathers
  Cleveland Bay 32
  Clydesdale *11*
  Fell 21
Fell breed **20–21**, *21*
Fjord breed **37**, *37*
floating, gait 5
Français, Selle 39
French saddle horse 39

gaits
  gliding walk 30
  Hanoverian 33
Gelderland 27
Godolphin 8
Groningen 27

H brand *33*
Hackney breed *36*, **37**
Haflinger breed **24–25**, *25*
Hanoverian breed **32–33**
heavy horse breeds 10–11, **38–39**
heavyweight hunter 10
Hebrides 36
Highland breed **14–15**, *15*
Holland 27
Holsteiner breed **39**
hunter
  heavyweight 10
  Thoroughbred 8

Icelandic breed **24**
Island Pony type 15

Jockey Club 35

Karst horses 28
Konik breed **37**

Lipizzaner breed **28–29**, *29*

Mainland Highland type 15

Marengo 4
McCue, Peter 7
miniature breeds 14, 39
Mongolia 36

Morgan breed **30–31**, *30*
Morgan Horse Club 31
Morgan, Justin 31
mulberry, colour 28
Mustangs **34–35**

Napoleon 4
New Forest
  breed **18–19**, *19*
  Breeding and Cattle Society 19
Newfoundland breed **37**
Nez Perce Indians 27, Nikolai Przewalski 36

Old English Black 10
Olympics, events 33
Overo 35

Paint breed **34–35**
Paint Horse Association, American 35
Palouse River 27
Percheron breed **38**, *38*
Peter McCue 7
Pinto breed **34–35**, *34*
Pinto Horse Association of America 35
ponies
  breeds **36–37**
  Dartmoor **16–17**
  Exmoor **16–17**
  Welsh **12–13**
Przewalski, Nikolai 36
Przewalski's horse breed **36**
pura espagnol 28

Quarter Horse breed **6–7**, *6*
Quarter Horse Association, American 35

Ranger 4
Rhum 15
riding and riders
  ponies, Welsh 13
Rogers, Roy 30
Romans, Ancient
  chariot racing 28
Russian cross 38

Saddlebred, American **39**, *39*
sections, Welsh 12
Selle Français breed **39**
Shetland **14–15**, *14*
Shire breed **10–11**, *10, 11*

shows and showing
  heavy horses 11
Spanish Riding School of Vienna 28
sports performance 27
spots 26
stallions, thoroughbred 8
Standardbred, American **38**

TB 9
Teke nomads 22
temperament 17
Tennessee Walking Horse breed **30–31**
Thoroughbred breed **8–9**, *8, 9*
  cross-breeds *4*, 9, 19, 33
'toad' eyes *17*
Tobiano 35
Tovero 35
Trakehner breed **38**
trekking 19, 20
Trigger 30
Turkmenistan 23
Turkoman Steppes 22

US army 27

vaulting 24
Vermont, USA 31
Vienna 28
Vikings 37
Virginian Islands 36

War
  First World 33
  Second World 10
warmblood 39
Washington, George 4
Wellington, Duke of 4
Welsh
  Cob *12*, 13
  mountain pony 12
  Pony and Cob Society 13
  pony breed **12–13**, *13*
  Stud Book 13
Western, quarter horse 7
World War I 33
World War II 10

Yili breed **38**

zebra stripes 36